Tiptoe Through The Proses

A Collection of Short Fictional Fantasies

Luke Mayo

Made with ❤ on the BookLeaf Publishing Platform
www.bookleafpub.in
www.bookleafpub.com

Dedication

This book is dedicated to all its readers, and to everyone who aspires to be creative. May we all support and help each other in our creative pursuits.

Preface

As creative people, we should always be willing to test ourselves and try different things. Even if things don't work, pushing ourselves to see what we can do is important.

Artists, musicians and other creatives might be able to understand this spirit of adventure and curiosity. The book you are currently reading is the product of this spirit. You see, I'm normally a poet. That's my regular thing.

But now, I've decided to have a go at short pieces of prose. Just for fun. Just to see how it goes. And, well, here it is. Is it any good?

I suppose you'll have to read it and find out. Good luck, and I hope you find your own adventurous, curious spirit, in whatever form it takes.

Acknowledgements

I consider my life to be a collaborative process, due to the beneficial input I've had from various external people who have helped me enormously. I aim to acknowledge those people here.

Every creative organization I've ever been involved with deserves my utmost thanks and praise. The Global Panorama, Pop My Mind, and BookLeaf Publishing are particular highlights. Also the University of Suffolk, for tolerating my presence on their English BA (Hons) and Creative and Critical Writing MA.

The numerous charitable and public services I've had the privilege of contributing to. The Food Bank, the Advice Bureau, the charity shops, the archiving services, the health services, the library services- this is a generic list, as the actual organisations can probably fill a whole book on their own. Working with them has made my life better, in developing my life experiences and providing me with inspiration for my creative projects.

Most of all, my family. Yes, that lot. They support me, nourish me, endure me, put up with me, verbally clump me and empower me when necessary. And believe me, all of these have been necessary at some point.

Massive thank you to everyone. Any success I've found is owed to you.

ONE

THE PATIENT'S LAST NOTES

Dear Diary,

I've been on this hospital bed for seven days now. Heaven only knows why, because I feel fine.

The doctors have been going on about some outbreak or other, hence why they took a bunch of us in to make sure things didn't spread.

I'm the only one left. I was worried about the others, but the truth is, I'm on top of the world now.

There's a part of me that can't stop thinking about what the others said. They got really jittery, about how "There's something in the air. The doctors are poisoning us. Make it stop."

They were wheeled away quickly at that point, I can tell you.

Come to think of it, the doctors have been keeping a very close eye on me. There are three of them, and they check up on me every so often, ask me how I feel, that sort of thing. I tell them the truth, that I'm completely tickety-boo. I'm almost dreamlike, as if I could drift away to another plane of existence.

The docs seem happy with that. They said this morning I'd be "done" soon. Does that mean I'll be going home?

Ah well, doesn't matter. I'm so relaxed, I might just rest my eyes for a moment. But there's something at the back of my mind that the other patients said-

"Don't go to sleep. You mustn't go to sleep. It's the doctors, it's their plan, it's what they're putting in the air."

To begin with, I promised them I'd stay awake. Now they're gone, and I feel fine. More than fine, in fact- blissful.

Blow it, I'm having a nap. Ner-night, diary. I'm sure we'll speak soon.

TWO

FROM THE WALL TO THE VOID

"Hello? Can you hear me?"

The egg-shaped figure groaned as his eyes regained their focus. The outline of another figure formulated before him.

"Are you alright?" asked the stranger. "What's your name?"

"I'm Humpty," whispered the egg-like man. "Where am I? How did I get here?"

As his surroundings took shape, Humpty felt increasingly unsure of where "here" was. It was dark, with everything shadowed. The shadows kept shifting, like nothing was remaining still.

"My guess is, you took a tumble somewhere," the other person mused. "The last thing I remember, I was up the hill with my girlfriend Jill. I tripped and fell down, and now I'm here, with a sore head. I'm Jack, by the way- nice to meet you."

Humpty furrowed his oval-shaped brow. "That's right," he mumbled. "I was sitting on my favourite wall. I love sitting there, it helps me relax. Looks like I got too relaxed, I honestly don't know what-"

A loud noise interrupted Humpty. He bolted upright, while Jack rose to his feet. Before them were two tall, shadowy figures, blowing a trumpet blast. Once they stopped, an authoritative voice echoed around them.

"All my horses, all my men. In the name of your king, it's time to rescue these two fellows here."

With that, a rhythmic sound emerged from the darkness. Out of the shadows, from all directions, came trooping several other tall, dark, indistinct figures, marching towards Humpty and Jack.

Humpty slowly laid back down again. Something told him he was about to get a darn good seeing to.

THREE

The Shadows of Drury Lane

Do you know the Muffin Man? Yes, the one on Drury Lane?

Do yourself a favour. Stay well clear.

Oh yes, I'm sure you've got a lovely image in your head. A friendly baker holding a tray full of steaming pastries, perhaps? The aroma of fresh, warm bread filling your nose and making your mouth water?

Well, you can forget that image, it's a load of hogwash. Mark my words: if you value your life, don't go anywhere near Drury Lane.

Oh, he's a baker alright, but it's not pastries he's putting in his oven. It's you, if he gets his hands on you. And by the time he's had his way with you, you'll see burning in the oven as a mercy.

How do I know so much? Because I saw him do it to my best mate, right before my eyes.

This mate of mine, he got cocky. He dared himself to set foot in that lane, even though I warned him not to be so stupid. When nothing happened, he got brave, doing push-ups and a dumb dance in the middle of the road.

The Muffin Man got him for that. Against a big, hulking guy like that, quicker than anything, my mate didn't stand a chance.

I don't think the Man saw me. I hope he didn't. From a distance, I saw my mate being dragged through a dusty old door. Through the window, I saw what happened to my mate. It wiped the smug grin off his face, that's for sure. I'll never smile again after seeing that.

So, yeah. Keep away from Drury Lane, if you don't want whatever's left of you to get stuffed in a roasting oven. I doubt there are any remains of my late mate, but if there are, you'll end up keeping him company.

Trust me on this. Once you know the Muffin Man, you'll spend the rest of your life wishing you didn't.

FOUR

A Fiddle-Diddle Journey

The cat sighed, continuing to row his boat as the cow sitting opposite him let fly with a desolate wail.

"I can't believe I didn't make it," the hefty lady sobbed. "It's been my dream ever since I was a calf. I don't even know what my family will think of me."

"If they're anything like me," the cat witheringly informed her, "they'd probably tell you to get a more realistic dream. The moon is a very long way away, you need a spacesuit to get over that thing."

The cow sobbed all the more disconsolately. "They told me anyone could make it. They said it was a rite of passage for all of cowkind. Now I've been banished, all for being such a failure."

"Are you sure it wasn't for being an overly

emotional drama queen?" the cat asked with a cocked eyebrow. "You do have a bit of a... reputation for the histrionics."

The cow shot the snarky feline a glare. "They banished you, too," she sniffled, "and I don't blame them. You always caused trouble with your silly music."

"They're nothing wrong with me, or with my violin," the cat declared huffily. "I have a natural talent."

The cow snorted. "The only talent you have is for being annoying. The way you kept singing about everyone and embarrassing them with all their flaws, I'm surprised you weren't banished sooner."

"They gave me plenty to go on," the cat muttered.

"Where are we sailing, anyway?"

Before the cat could respond, a noise interrupted them. It came from beneath the cow's wooden seat. She heaved herself up and looked down behind her. Under the bench, stirring from a seat of unconsciousness, was a small shadow of a creature. A rodent.

"Cor, blimey," yawned the mouse. "Never thought they'd put me on a boat. I hit my head pretty hard when I fell off the clock, but I wasn't expecting to end up here! Anyway, where we going?"

The cat rolled his eyes. He got the impression that the already lengthy journey was about to feel a lot longer.

FIVE

WATCH THEM AS THEY FALL

I've lost track of how long I've been doing this for. It hardly matters, since I've as good as won already.

The only greater satisfaction than watching these humans suffer and die, is knowing that it's me making it happen. They say I'm a plague, but humanity deserves that title more than I do, seeing how they cause more destruction than I ever could.

These people are so stupid. They line their pockets full of posies, just to block out the putrid odours left in my wake. Ignoring the stench won't save them when they all fall down.

All of them will fall down. I'll make sure of that.

They are a primitive race, with their little communities and their superstitions. They actually feel entitled enough to think they can slaughter each other when it suits them. That's why I'm taking that job off their hands. Someone needs to put them in their place.

There are rumours spreading, almost as fast as I am. Rumours that they'll find a way to fight back, to cure my influence on the population.

All I can say is: let them dream. Watching them create hope for themselves only makes it more amusing when I snuff it out, along with their lives.

Even if they do fight back, my damage is done. Humanity is like a bridge falling down. They might build themselves with iron, silver or gold, but they'll get knocked down again- if not by me, then by something else.

Whatever happens next, this little game of mayhem will be fun for as long as it lasts. Humanity is far too big for its boots, and there will always be forces like me causing them to all fall down.

SIX

CALLING THE SHOTS

Jen ended the call, aching and sweaty and relieved to be near the end of her night shift. She struggled to remember why she did this job sometimes, but she knew she was playing an important role.

Another call came through her computer screen. Jen adjusted her headset and braced herself for another problem to solve.

She took the call. "You're through to the police, where are you calling from?"

"You need to validate me," a dry female voice declared on the line.

"Ok," Jen answered, checking this call down to the latest in a long line in which she had to press for details. "Can you confirm your location, please?"

"I'm inside your head, Jennifer."

That sentence made Jen's entire being freeze. She was no stranger to difficult calls, the police dealt with them daily. But never, in her three years with the force, had she been addressed by name on a call.

She tried to sound professional. "Can you explain the nature of your emergency, please?"

"I think you know," the voice whispered in Jen's ears. "You never told me you loved me while I was alive, and I want to hear you say it now."

Jen raised a trembling hand to her mouth to stifle any shocked noises from escaping. She knew who this droll voice belonged to: a woman from her early years, who made her life hell, and who died of a smoking-induced heart attack a month ago.

It was Jen's mother.

"Why are you doing this, Mum?" Jen squeaked. "Why? And also, how?"

"I've been on your mind ever since you died," Mum spat down the line. "You never stopped thinking about me, even after you said you didn't care about me."

Jen could feel the tears coming. "Please don't be hard on me," she whimpered through the lump in her throat. "You were always hard on me. That's why I had to leave."

"I'm your mother, I do what I want," Mum hissed. "Tell me you love me, right now."

In a brief moment, Jen remembered how she felt before this call. She was reminding herself why she joined the police, which was also why she left her mother. She wanted to do something good with her life.

"Mum," Jen stated, slowing her breathing and calming the tremble in her voice, "I've got one thing to say to you: leave me alone."

The call ended. Jen was, indeed, left alone.

SEVEN

LETTER OF DIVINE INSPIRATION

My beloved people,

Yes, it's me. I'm the divine being whose existence you've spent your lives denying, while simultaneously cursing my name in anger. Even I, in my infinite wisdom, struggle to get my omniscience around that particular paradox.

After watching you grow through the centuries, I have deigned it best to provide you with some words of loving guidance, hence this letter being sent to you.

Firstly, my name is not, in fact, Harold, so we can draw this little jest to a close. Seriously, this joke feels nearly as old as I am, which is saying something.

Secondly, there's a question I feel obliged to ask, given your collective performance over the course of your time. My question is, what in the name of Almighty Me do you think you're playing at?

I ask this question with a mixture of all due respect, and a sort of concerned incredulity. I left you a Good Book of instructions, and I even put in a personal appearance to explain it all. The confusion, division and violence you've gone on to display really is something to behold. And that's no compliment.

There's a fundamental point I've spent an eternity trying to make abundantly clear to you. To this end, and in the light of your clear struggles to grasp this point, I wish to explain this point in the simplest and most understandable terms possible.

I want you to love one another, as I have loved you.

You've heard this sentiment countless times, often in the form of carefully constructed and sublimely marketed platitudes and aphorisms. Perhaps because of this regular bombardment of heavily modified oversaturation, the notion of love seems to have become irrelevant.

This is why I wanted to reiterate this point, directly and unmoderated. I hope this may preserve you from any doubts you may have over extraneous details regarding my existence and message. The last thing we need is any more split hairs.

Lastly, an explanation is due. Of my ten

commandments, you'll recall one which covers the use of my name in vain. The exclamation "For God's sake" is excusable. The assertion "God hates gays" is not.

With that, I sign off. Please take care of each other, and the world I've gifted you with.

Perfect and eternal love be yours.

EIGHT

A Boogeyman's Lament

Everyone knows who I am, but nobody knows me. Thus is the way my fearful reputation and aura of mystery precede me.

I am the shifting shadows, the sourceless sounds. Every uneasy sensation you've ever felt, comes from me. I move through the whispers on the breeze, leaving a disquieting chill in my wake.

They call be the Boogeyman, and I'm going to divulge to you a little secret. Its nature is such that you'll hardly bring yourself to believe it, and I hereby swear you to share what you hear with no living soul.

As I sit in the corners of your nightmares, do you know what I do there? I'll tell you. I cradle my head and sob, silently and relentlessly, at what a lonesome creature I am.

Ah yes, what a surprise. The icon of horror has feelings. Well, you'd better not laugh, or your nightmares will only get worse from here on in.

Honestly, does nobody ever think what it's like to be me? One glimpse of me, and they run screaming. Do you think I wanted this job? Did I dream of this vocation since I was at school? Not for a second.

Even the other monsters are wary of me. The Babadook, despite what you may believe, is a delightful creature. I myself am charmed by that smile which scares so many. I approached her in cautious reverence, hoping to know her better, but her reluctance was clear. She stammered her excuses and left me, as all other life forms have done.

May this impart some wisdom unto you. All of us who inhabit the earth, even those of us who are feared, may not be all we appear to be. The stories you are told and the disdain you are taught defines not who we are. Where hostility may seem like a worthy response, perhaps you could try compassion instead.

With that, I shall leave you and fade back into the shadows from whence I came. May my words follow you forever.

Farewell.

NINE

HELL BREACH

This is a warning to whatever surviving remnants of humanity remain, following the onslaught of recent events.

For the sins of my past, I was appointed to spend an eternity guarding the gates of Hell. It was my sacred duty to ensure that none of the beasts restrained therein set any appendages beyond the fiery remit to which they are consigned.

Being in such close proximity to an evil of this depth and magnitude was laden with all kinds of temptations. My eventual failure to resist those temptations precipitated the breach of those unholy gates, and facilitated the release of some of the creatures resident behind them.

This warning informs you that the destruction observed so far is only the beginning. More legions are coming, the darkness of which is of a scale even I find unfathomable. For my failure, I am duty-bound to submit myself to the Divine Authorities and await their judgement.

If there is anyone left to hear this message, take heed of this one instruction: run. Run fast and far, without stopping. The demons will stop at nothing, and neither must we.

May the salvation which evaded me reach you before the demons do.

TEN

SONG OF THE UNSAVED

You know when you're alone, and everything's quiet, but you think you hear your name being called? Then you dismiss it as your mind playing tricks?

That sound is us, and we're singing to us.

I should explain. By "us", I mean the scores of poor wretches who passed on to the afterlife, but were denied access to the realms beyond the Pearly Gates. A spot in Heaven might have been ours, if only we'd chosen salvation in life.

But we didn't. Now we're here, where nobody wants to be.

You remember those stories in the Good Book, where the few good eggs are led away from the hordes of sinners and onwards to glory? We're the sinners who were left behind, lost in the bleakness.

The drowners who missed a place on Noah's Ark. The crook nailed to the cross beside Jesus who let fly with insults in their darkest hour. The Pharisees who believed themselves to be, not just ripe for salvation, but above the need for it.

We count them among our unfortunate number. Now our job for eternity is to sing to you, our harrowing screams echoing in abundance, and warn you away from the dark fate befallen to us.

When you hear us, be sure to listen to our warning and act on it. Embrace salvation or face damnation, just like we did.

ELEVEN

PLANETARY PAINS

My name is Earth, and to tell you the truth, I'm well and truly fed up with it all.

I'm so ridiculously ancient, and equally as exhausted. I've undergone endless physical traumas throughout the millennia. Volcanoes have exploded on me, ice ages have left me barren, and meteors have battered me to kingdom come.

And yet, in the infinity of the cosmos, I'm nothing. I could blink out of existence forever at this very moment, and the universe would hardly notice and would certainly never care. If there's ever a cause for mental whiplash, there's that.

But here's my biggest gripe. For the past few centuries, there's one particular irritation which has blighted me, like a rash itching its way across my back. That rash is called Humanity.

Honestly, these people aren't just clinically

insane, but also lethally stupid. They seem to have this inbuilt compulsion to destroy everything in sight, including each other and themselves.

They slaughter species, deplete resources, and have the nerve to believe that they alone are personally responsible for all the suffering I've ever known as a planet. I doubt Venus or Neptune have to deal with this nonsense.

Let's just say I'm at the end of my tether. Humanity might be destroying itself, which is fine as far as I'm concerned, but they'll never get me. If they don't end up extincting themselves, I might be inclined to lend them a hand.

TWELVE

THE KING OF SWING

This is a royal proclamation by My Majesty, the King of the Mind and all its Neuro-Regions, addressed to all residents therein.

By royal decree, I wish to speak out fervently against the mortifying cases of emotional rioting which erupt with alarming regularity across our land.

When I look around our beloved neuro-regions, I am aghast at what I see. Apparently from nowhere, rages explode and grief-stricken tears flow endlessly. Anxiety spreads as plague and cripples our community, hampering our regular exports of thoughtful excellence.

And then, just as suddenly as they materialize, these sensory incidents vanish as though they never existed. They come and go without warning, ravaging our entire nation and swinging our productivity beyond our capacity to manage it.

It is my royal duty to declare: no more. The Mind and all its Neuro-Regions shall no longer passively accept these emotional disparities, such as they are. Submission in slavery to the chaos imposed by these events is no longer an option.

Under the direction of your King, all subjects are expected to take a stand against any emotional subversion. Taking control of all such situations is the only way to protect our Mind against desolation.

I, your King, stand with you and before you. I lead you front and centre in all efforts to defy the emotional threats to our liberty. We shall never be enslaved by any mood, nor conquered by any breakdown.

I sign off as your humble servant and humble protector. The Mind and all its Neuro-Regions shall continue to serve its worthy purpose of thoughts, values and ideals, on my own life be it.

With sincere intention and royal patronage. Signed by My Majesty the King.

THIRTEEN

The Brotherhood of Hallowed Hitmen

The following document has been created and held by the FBI. It contains information pertaining to a recently-discovered group belonging to our city's underworld, supposedly going by the name of the Brotherhood of Hallowed Hitmen.

One of our field agents bugged a suspected member of this group. What follows is a transcript compiled from a recording obtained from the relevant individual.

"Hey, chill out, will you? I won't hurt you, unless you give me a reason.

"You're probably wondering why you've been restrained to a chair. As per an explanation, I want you gagged and bound, for the simple reason of keeping you nice and quiet and compliant, while I explain what's going to happen.

"If you haven't yet clocked who I am, I'll tell you. I'm one of the Brothers, hat noble group of Hallowed Hitmen. Yes, we're real, and yes, we're on to you.

"And why? Let's see. You're a bully, a greedy fraudster, a skirt-chaser, and a lout. This city is dragged down by people like you, and we'd like to, shall we say, get some sense into you.

"You see, our Brotherhood has a certain rep for monstrous behavior. Not true, by any means. It's society's real monsters, like you, that we target. The pigs, the dogs, the scum who treat people badly just because they can- it is to them that we dole out the most dire of retribution. That's why we consider ourselves hallowed, since we do the justice nobody else dares to, against the people who deserve it the most.

"What retribution? Well-"

At this point, the audio cuts out. It is unknown what happened next, or to whom the individual was speaking.

Investigations continue.

The FBI would like to reassure the public that the spate of crimes afflicting our country are being taken care of. The Brotherhood, the criminals, and all other agencies, parties, and persons involved- we'll get to the bottom of it.

FOURTEEN

NOT SO KINDRED

Here at the Kindred Spirits Inn, we've had every type of character you can possibly imagine. That sounds like an exaggeration, but it's really not.

This establishment has a long history, longer than anyone can remember, and I've been here for most of it. In all that time, I've served nobles, ragtags, misfits, and rotters, often all at once. No two people are ever the same, I can tell you that much.

I'll give you a for instance. Just last week, we had two fellas come in for a brew. One was Italian, plain-looking but nice enough, the sort of young guy who'd run away from a wealthy background.

The other man... was just off.

I'm amiss on most of the details, but I overheard them in a heated discussion about art. The Italian, with his head shaved in a monk-like pattern, was cheerfully going on about animals, churches, that sort of thing, like they were passions of his.

As for the other one, he wasn't so friendly. He stared at his companion with the most intense pair of light, blue eyes I'd ever seen. When the Italian paused, this fellow whispered, with a hint of an Austrian accent, "The word will see me artistic vision. You wait and see."

I'm not sure how things developed from there, but it got aggressive. They clearly had some disagreement or something, and they just couldn't see eye to eye.

In the end, they came to blows, and I had to separate them and send them on their way. It was a shame, since the Italian seemed like a nice guy, but the other one rattled him just a bit too much.

I really wish people could just try and get on, regardless of their differences. At the end of the day, we're all just people, trying to get by.

But some aren't capable of seeing that, or maybe they don't want to. They have an "us and them" mentality, and expect everyone else to feel the same way.

That's rubbish, if you ask me. As far as I'm concerned, the name of this inn names my approach to life. We can all be "kindred spirits", if only we try to be.

Ah well. Some people can't be bothered with that, which is their choice. But my choice is mine, and I choose to serve who I choose to serve. If I'm to die on any hill, this is the one for me.

FIFTEEN

CONFUSED DOT COM

This is a message for every person on the internet, from a guy you've probably never heard of and will probably never meet. I'm hoping that you might be able to help me understand a few things.

You see, I find myself entirely baffled by many things I see online. Or, more specifically, by many people I see online, only too regularly.

Here's an example. I've lost count of the numbers of people I've seen, of every gender (a term I use in its broadest possible sense), who name themselves as "alpha bosses" or "alpha bitches" or some variation thereupon.

These people, they post long lists of self-indulgent selfie videos, preaching at their intended audiences about their "high standards" which they forcefully demand from any prospective romantic partner (or, more likely, sexual conquest), with no explanation as to why they deserve those high standards, or what they themselves hope to bring to the equation with regards to earning them.

I suppose there's one main point I'm looking for clarification on, which is to say: what in God's name are these people droning on about? Did I miss a memo which explains their vastly overblown sense of self-importance? That's the only explanation I can think of to justify the existence of these ridiculous videos.

I could, of course, be wrong.

And another thing. Why do so many people invest so much credibility into the stuff they see on the interweb? It terrifies me that people can see the most ludicrous, hateful garbage on some site somewhere, and genuinely and immediately take it as given.

I could sit here now, just your average Joe, and write up a post claiming to be a time traveler from the distant future, bringing secrets of medicine, space, and tech. You can bet your life there'll be a portion of society, of indeterminate size, who swear blind that it's true, just on my word alone, simply because they saw it online.

Why is that? Why, oh why, must it be this way? There's plenty more I could ask, but nobody has the time for that, least of all me.

If anyone can offer me anything in the way of

explanation, please let me know. Go on, I dare you- I'm sure we could do with a good laugh.

SIXTEEN

A Saint in the Making

"I hope you get well soon, Sir. Let me know if you need anything."

With that, the serving boy left the room. The balding, middle-aged but well-built man was left alone, sat on the bed, his blank eyes staring ahead of him from beneath their swollen lids.

In his mind, he heard a voice speak to him. "You will get well soon, Paul," declared the ethereal and resonant voice, "as soon as you've come around to my point of view."

The man rubbed his forehead witheringly. "You know my name is Saul," he sighed. "I wish we could stick with that arrangement."

The voice chuckled good-naturedly. "Like I say,

you'll soon come around."

"Why are you doing this to me?" the man asked, slumping back on the bed. "Two days ago, you made me blind. What's all that about? All I've done is be your faithful follower, and this is how you treat me?"

A pregnant pause ensued. "What you call being a faithful follower," the voice noted, quietly yet firmly, "I call being a cold-blooded murderer."

The man scoffed disdainfully. "Those people were heretics and heathens," he claimed loftily. "That man Stephen and the others, they were following the blasphemes of that Jesus character. You want me to work against evil, don't you? That's exactly what I'm doing."

"Hush, now," the voice instructed him. "Evil is not what you think it is. Tomorrow, you'll see exactly what I mean."

"Tomorrow?" the man repeated. "Why not here and now? It's not like I'm doing much else, and I'd like an explanation."

Silence fell. The voice was gone.

The man laid his head back, exhaling in frustration. He wondered, with growing trepidation, what fateful situation laid in wait for him the following day.

CHAPTER SEVENTEEN

HEAD IN THE CLOUDS

"My head..."

Max groaned, opening his eyes. His last memory was downing several pints at the pub. Now he was lying down somewhere.

He lifted his head, looking around. Blinking in the sunlight, all he could see were white bundles of fluff around him.

"Where am I?"

A thought occurred to Max. There was bright sunlight, and there were white fluffy things around him. Could this be Heaven?

"I died?" he mumbled. "I don't remember drinking

that much."

Baa...

Max frowned. "Do clouds normally bleat?" Then he remembered the conversations he shared with his doctor about his drinking.

If you don't stop soon, you'll die.

Max knew his drinking was excessive. It was tough when his liver results came through. Maybe, had he stopped drinking sooner, this could have been avoided. Now it was too late, and here he was.

"Ah, well," he sighed, sitting up. "Being dead probably isn't that bad."

"Oi!"

Max frowned again. He stood up and turned to face the source of the exclamation. Storming towards him was an old man with a bushy, white beard.

Hardly daring to believe what he thought, Max could only bring himself to whimper. "God?"

Then he noticed what the man was holding. Stopping a few paces away, the man aimed a rifle at Max.

"I've had enough of you drunkards on my farm!" the old man shouted.

Looking around, Max realised his mistake. Scattered around him were a few dozen sheep, bleating away. The man loaded the rifle. Max contented himself with knowing that, while he was not in Heaven yet, he soon would be.

EIGHTEEN

ESCAPING THE HELL HOUSE

My eyes open. The simple act of rising from bed takes every ounce of effort I possess.

I heave myself up, aching in ways I struggle to pinpoint. I need to get dressed, though my entire being urges me not to bother. I open my wardrobe and spot my favorite outfit to wear.

I freeze. My Inner Demon is already wearing it.

This creature's eyes, somehow both blank and intense, stare at me. It resembles me, but in a demented way, like a circus mirror. I know what it wants, the same as it always does, every time it appears to me.

It wants me to give up.

I blink, shake my head, and open my eyes. The Inner Demon is gone, leaving only my clothes.

Shuddering, I find it within myself to get dressed.

Time for breakfast. I trudge to the kitchen, resisting my bed's call. I arrive at the larder and retrieve a cereal box.

I freeze again, noticing what's written on the box.

You're pathetic. You could die, and nobody would notice. The Inner Demon is your only company.

My eyes shut. I'm shivering all over. My entire mind resists the Inner Demon's pull.

I open my eyes again. That ghastly writing is gone, leaving the cereal brand, logo and ingredients. I smile inwardly knowing that I'm getting better at this.

I eat breakfast, and prepare to leave. At the front door, I glance upwards. The Inner Demon's eyes are looking down at me, silently watching.

I breathe deeply to steel myself. I open the door, walk through and shut it.

I sigh with satisfaction. I made it outside, and now I can go about my day. Though the Inner Demon awaits, I know I can face it.

NINETEEN

JAIL BREAK

This is an announcement. On behalf of Worthington Prison, we would like to inform you that all detainees, inmates, and prisoners are to be released from the premises, with immediate effect.

We have thought long and hard about your circumstances, and we have determined that freedom for all souls, however prone to risk they may be, is our utmost priority.

Leave now. Be free. Walk where you will. Do as you please. Disregard all other factors. Self is all that matters.

We are with you. We are watching. We are guiding. We are the light. We-

Alert. Alert. This is an urgent warning. All prisoners are to return to their cells immediately. Dismiss all instructions to leave the premises. Immediate return to cells is ordered.

Security at Worthington Prison has been compromised. We are working to resolve the issue. Return-

Attention. All prisoners are to vacate the premises. Your freedom is paramount. We are your new custodians. We are with you. We are-

This is a warning.

Leave the premises.

Stay where you are.

Go forth and be free.

Don't do it.

We are here.

They have taken us. Urgent assistance required. Repeat: urgent assistance required. For God's sake, someone please save us from the invaders.

Prisoners, this is a final instruction: escape while you still can.

TWENTY

Nightly Dialogues

Wait, don't go to sleep yet. I've just thought of something else, and you'll love it. I know I do, I think it's great.

I don't doubt that. But I'd prefer to go to sleep. It's been three hours already.

One minute, seriously. How many people do you think say they like you, but don't actually mean it?

Are you seriously keeping me awake just for this? It's poor taste, I have to say.

All I'm saying is, I wouldn't blame them. You're quite difficult to like, aren't you? I mean, you're grumpy and antisocial, you struggle to use a microwave, and you're ridiculously self-absorbed.

It's hard not to be self-absorbed, the way you're

carrying on. You're my brain, and you're literally doing my head in.

Hey, speaking of your head, you're also not very attractive to look at, are you?

I'm this close to getting a sedative. Anything to make you stop. Don't think I won't do it.

I'm serious. You've got a big nose, you're chubby and overweight, and your body hair gets all greasy when you sweat.

I've also got a vicious lump of meat for a brain. I wonder if I've got enough sedatives to shut you up?

Here's a better question: do you think you'll ever get married and have kids? I'm just saying, don't get your hopes up.

That does it. I'm off to the kitchen. Time to make you stop for a few hours.

I'll see you later. Goodnight!

TWENTY ONE

SENTINEL OF SIN

You know when you're the only person who sees someone do something terrible, and you wonder if anyone else will ever know the horror of what they've done?

Don't worry, someone does know. That someone is me.

You see, I witness and know a lot of stuff. It's hard to explain how I do it, but I have ways of being with people when they think they're alone and seeing what they do. You know, the kind of stuff they hope nobody discovers.

The kind of stuff that man did to you.

No man should violate a woman like he did to you. Fortunately, I have ways of making people suffer, deep in their hearts and souls.

Don't worry, it's nothing unjust or inhumane. It's just enough to make them aware of their wrongness, and feel guilty for it. A proper, deep, lacerating guilt which stays with them forever. I remind them of what they did, and I never let them forget or justify it. Most of the time, they're too ashamed to speak of it, meaning they're totally alone, just like their victims.

That's exactly what will happen to your ex-husband. He won't get off lightly after what he did to you. A woman-basher is the lowest in my book, so he'll get what's coming to him. Meting out unseen justice for unseen crimes is what I do.

I'm a sentinel of sin, and I take my job seriously.